9.99

D0500981

COME TO THE CRADLE

MICHAEL CARD

ILLUSTRATIONS BY FRED WARTER

Sparrow Press
Nashville, Tennessee

© 1993 Michael Card

All rights reserved. Written permission must be secured from the publisher to use or reproduce any part of this book, except for brief quotations in critical reviews or articles.

Published 1993 in Nashville, Tennessee, by Sparrow Press,
and distributed in Canada by Christian Marketing Canada, Ltd.

Printed in the United States of America

97 96 95 94 93   5 4 3 2 1

Library of Congress Cataloging-in-Publication Data

Card, Michael 1957-
    Come to the cradle / Michael Card.
      p.   cm.
    ISBN 0-917143-24-8 : $12.95
    1. Parents– Prayer-books and devotions – English. 2. Spiritual life – Christianity.
I. Title.
BV4845.C37 1993
242' .645–dc20

                            93-10325
                            CIP

All songs by Michael Card
©1993 Birdwing Music (a div. of The Sparrow Corp.) and BMG Songs, Inc., All rights on behalf of Birdwing Music admin. by BMG Songs, Inc. All Rights Reserved. International Copyright Secured.

Except:
"Come to the Cradle" by Michael Card & Phil Naish
©1993 Birdwing Music (a div. of The Sparrow Corp.) and BMG Songs, Inc./Davaub Music. All rights on behalf of Birdwing Music and Davaub Music admin. by BMG songs, Inc. All Rights Reserved. International Copyright Secured.

"Lullaby For Jesus" and "Light of the World" by Michael Card
©1982 Mole End Music (All rights controlled and administered by The Sparrow Corporation). All Rights Reserved. International Copyright Secured.

"Angel by Your Bed," "The Love That I Bear," "A Gift of Life" and "Oh, Father of Jesus" by Michael Card and Scott Brasher
©1993 Birdwing Music (a div. of The Sparrow Corp.) and BMG Songs, Inc./ Mole End Music. All rights on behalf of Birdwing Music and Mole End Music admin. by BMG Songs, Inc. All rights Reserved. International Copyright Secured.

All lyrics used by permission.

Design by Brenda Whitehill

he cradle calls us to come away from the busyness of the world—to rediscover the holy, unhurried life of a child, and to discover that as we pour ourselves into the lives of our little ones, life overflows in return.

For the cry of a baby in the middle of the night is not simply a summons to change a diaper—it contains within it more than our ears can hear. It is a call to leave the cozy self-interest of our warm beds; to come, saying no to a thousand voices that tell us to remain where we are comfortable. It is a call to come away from ourselves. No one who has ever heeded this call will tell you it was in vain.

As we sit and sing to our children in the night, to calm their fears and put them to sleep, we sing to ourselves as well. If we choose our songs with care we wake up to the sound of the words, that we might be for our daughters and sons all they need us to be—and that we might open our eyes to all they are to us.

It is our calling to teach our children about the realities of our world. But it is the natural gift of our children to reintroduce us to the realities of their world, of the world each of them carries around inside themselves, of the world that carries each one of them. Our world is filled with warnings and worries. Theirs, filled with wonder and the divine wisdom of innocence. It is a wisdom and freedom that come, paradoxically, from not knowing—the same sort of wisdom Adam and Eve possessed before the fall, before they set foot into the world we know, our world.

So come to the cradle of your child and pray that you might wake up as they nod off to sleep. Come learn simplicity, naiveté, simple trusting faith. Pray for them and over them and with them, asking the Father to be with them as they grow to adulthood, and asking the Father to be with you, as by His grace you become a child again.

Come to the cradle

Come and find peace

Alone in the cradle

Simplicity sleeps

Behold, perfect wisdom

So gentle and mild

In the innocent, upward

Trusting glance of a child

Come hear the call

Of sweet sighs in the dark

Their touch is tender

It touches your heart

The bustle and business

Lasts year after year

But this little baby

Won't always be here

Come to the cradle

Come and find peace

Alone in the cradle

Simplicity sleeps

Behold, perfect wisdom

So gentle and mild

In the innocent, upward

Trusting glance of a child

When God gives a gift

He wraps it up in a child

He made them

Loves them

So wondrously wild

And so you are chosen

And called out for prayer

So come to the cradle

He waits for you there

COME TO THE CRADLE

Sleep in the Bow

MATTHEW 8:23ff

Sweet Jesus, You slept
Through the storm in the bow
Through lightning, through thunder
You slumbered, but how?
You totally trusted Your Father
That's how
You slept through the storm in the bow

Were You simply fearless
A sleeper so sound
That You could find rest
With a storm all around

Was it simple trust in
Your Father that made
The danger seem
Like a charade

Sweet Jesus, the storms
Of this life rage and howl
So sometimes for little ones
Sleep's disallowed

Raise up now and speak
That these storms may be gone
And make my waves calm now
From darkness till dawn

Sweet Jesus, You slept
Through the storm in the bow
Through lightning, through thunder
You slumbered, but how?
You totally trusted Your Father
That's how
You slept through the storm in the bow

9

hen my children play, it is most often in childlike imitation of adult roles. Katie is the dancer, the teacher, the mommy. Will is always and only the archaeologist, digging for dinosaurs. They are so busy and yet never consumed with busyness. Their play never degenerates into work.

What are they trying to teach me? Could my work become playful imitation of what I see my Father doing? Could I learn from them the secret of lifting my work up to the plane of play?

Work, even a little work, exhausts me, takes away from me. Play, even a little play, pours something back in. Work has to do with anxiety, with doing a good job. Play springs from inexhaustible joy. Since it is play, after all, what does it matter if it's a symphony or a scribble? The point of work is to finish. The point of play is to *not* finish, or at least to draw it out until bedtime. Work is rooted in a curse. Play comes closer to what Eden was all about.

Play usually begins with a gift: A toy. An empty box. A sheet of paper and some crayons. Or perhaps even a child and the eyes to see.

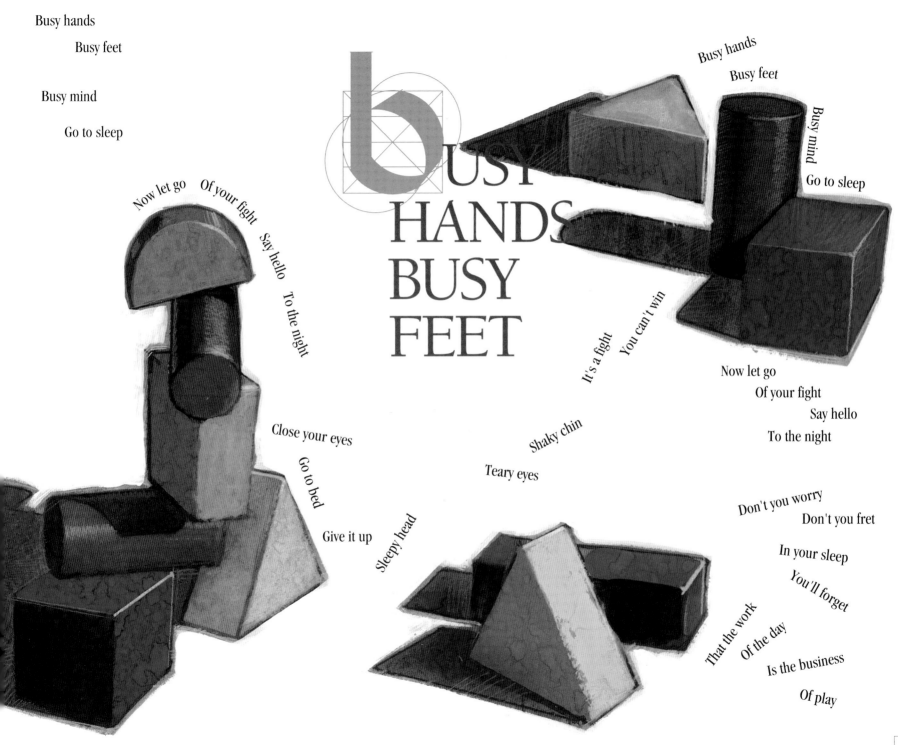

Busy hands

Busy feet

Busy mind

Go to sleep

Busy hands

Busy feet

Busy mind

Go to sleep

Now let go   Of your fight   Say hello   To the night

It's a fight   You can't win

Now let go

Of your fight

Say hello

To the night

Close your eyes

Go to bed

Give it up

Shaky chin

Teary eyes

Sleepy head

Don't you worry

Don't you fret

In your sleep

You'll forget

That the work

Of the day

Is the business

Of play

bUSY
HANDS
BUSY
FEET

Albert is a friend I know
Who walks a shuffling way
And you must learn to
read his face
For he hasn't much to say
But he carries 'round
inside himself
A knowledge he gives free
If you look through,
not at his life
A whole new world inside
you'll see

When a window is
a mirror
You see two ways
at one time
You look outside and see
the land
The mountains left
to climb
But also you can
see inside
Your face suspended there
Behold your face and see
your place
And understand why
you are here

WHEN A WINDOW

 IS A MIRROR

FOR ALBERT MOSS

Each time I gaze upon
this boy
There's something
moves inside
I see my own deformities
No longer need to hide

And through his life
I look upon
My life a different way
This freedom that
he gives for free
Means so much more
than I can say

When a window is a
mirror
You see two ways at one
time
You look outside and see
the land
The mountains left to
climb
But also you can see
inside
Your face suspended there
Behold your face and see
your place
And understand why you
are here

And Albert offers, at no
charge
The hope one life can
bring
But what he freely gives us
all
Has cost him nearly
everything

Once upon a time there was a man, born blind, who though he had never seen the light of day, was so deeply good that his life became a light to others, so that through him they were able to see.

Once upon a time there was a deaf woman. Never in her long life had she heard a note of music, nor the song of a bird. But because of the simplicity of her heart, her life became a song, and the music of herself meant more than anyone could ever sing.

Once upon a time there was a little girl who was poor and alone. Except for the charity of one kind man she would have starved. And yet, though the man was rich, it was feeding the little girl that truly satisfied his hunger. And if it had not been for her, he would have starved.

Once there was a crippled boy. He could not take a step on his own and so had to be carried by his father everywhere he went. Even as the boy grew, the strain of his weight was never seen on his father's face. Whenever he was asked how he managed the burden of his son, the father would take a deep breath and answer, "Because the truth is I am the burden my son bears, and it is he who has carried me to the place I am today."

ver since the big thunderstorm, Katie had been afraid of the dark. Even when the night was calm outside she would worry about lightning and the sound of the wind. Her mother and father did the best they could to comfort her tears and calm her fears, but in the end she would always cry herself to sleep.

One night, as she lay in bed determined not to break into tears, Katie heard a rustling sound. Over in the corner she heard the sound of chalk scratching against the blackboard.

For some unknowable reason, Katie was more curious than afraid, and so she slid out from between the sheets and tiptoed over to the light switch. The lights came on brighter than she expected (as they always do when you turn them on in the middle of the night).

In the corner, beside the doll house, she saw that the little blackboard was now leaning against her babies' cradle. Written in beautifully shaped letters was the message, "FEAR NOT."

Barely able to read, Katie sounded out each word until their meaning came together in her mind.

"F-e-e-e-a-r-r-r n-o-o-o-t-t-t," she whispered to herself. "F-e-e-a-r n-o-o-t. Oh! Fear not . . . fear not."

She thought that perhaps her mother had crept into the room and written the message, but these didn't look like the letters Mommy usually wrote on the chalkboard. They curled back on themselves and ended with lovely flourishes.

Night after night the message appeared until Katie became so preoccupied with it she forgot about being afraid. She asked her parents and brothers if they were guilty, but they all denied writing it.

One night there came a furious storm. The rain battered against the roof with a vengeance, and lightning flashes lit up Katie's room.

She lay in bed, trying to ignore the storm, repeating to herself over and over the special message: "Fear not, fear not, fear not."

All at once the lightning struck so close to the house that the windows rattled. In the flash of light Katie thought she saw someone kneeling in the corner of her room, beside the doll house, writing on the chalkboard. Each time the lightning flashed she could make out the image better and better until it became forever fixed in her mind.

"Who are you?" she whispered from underneath the covers.

The shadowy shape looked over and whispered kindly, "Fear not."

For the rest of her life, whenever she needed it most, Katie recalled the image of the gentle man kneeling in the corner of her room. Sometimes, when she was especially afraid, she even thought she could hear his voice whispering to her, "Fear not."

Fear Not

ANGEL BY YOUR BED

MATTHEW 18:10

There won't always be diapers
And bars round your bed
And soft angel hair
Making curls round your head
But the one who keeps watch
Through the dark of the night
Will never forsake
Ever ready to fight

Dream of the angel
Who waits by your bed
Let sleep draw the curtain
Inside, sleepy head
As he watches and waits
For your safety and care
Do blind sleeping eyes
See him there

Look up, see the face
That will watch all your life
The gift of his presence
A presence of light
He stands straight and strong
And so awesome in might
And know he'll be here
All your life

emember the anticipation of seeing that somehow-familiar face for the first time, of hearing the first cry, of counting fingers and toes. Recall the joy of delivery, of being delivered of a baby.

For moms, the presence has been real for some time. For us dads it doesn't seem real until we see shadows on the screen of an ultrasound or hear the heartbeat or perhaps feel a kick in the night. Breathtaking is the thought that the baby within is a spirit, a soul from the beginning, and not, as some believe, from the first breath. A presence. A person. A living soul.

This is not merely a fetus that inhabits the womb. This is another soul, a being more spirit than flesh, created in God's image. And just as God is Spirit and Truth, so there is something true about a baby, even as there is something true about bearing one.

But after a baby is born, he or she still must be borne. And while a mother may be delivered of her child, she never completely gets the child out of her. Though her babes may outgrow her arms, she will always hold them in her heart.

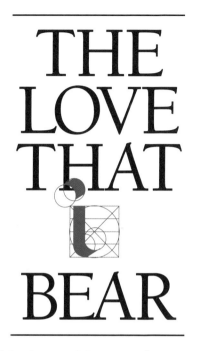

I sing of the life that I bear
I sing to the one who's inside of me
Whose face is familiar
Though I've never seen
Whose life lies ahead
Like a wonderful dream

I sing of the love that I bear
I sing to the Spirit indwelling me
Alive deep inside me
As surely, I know
As my baby
Is living and grows

Passion and pain
Come together the same
As the flesh and the blood
Come by way of one love
Sing then to life
And of love come alive
So all that is darkness
Will die

f life is a battle, as the Bible indicates, then all who believe are warriors for His sake. But if this is true, then we must be something else as well. We are the trainers for the younger generation. We are drill sergeants for the Kingdom, for the next army of warriors.

In the military, the drill sergeant is usually the most zealous soldier. In movies we've seen him yelling at the top of his lungs at the frightened and confused recruits, because he knows that wars are lost and won on the drilling field. Their outcome depends on the training he provides. He instructs when to flee and when to fight. He counsels on the best tactics to use against the enemy. And most importantly, he teaches the recruits to become familiar with the implements of war.

Perhaps in the past some Christian parents have taken this pattern to the extreme, raising real soldiers and not true Kingdom warriors. But that is no reason to discard the analogy. Everyone who is a part of a family—aunts, uncles, grandparents and friends—is called to be part of this discipling process. And as is true in all areas of Christian life, the way is paradoxically reversed.

Our drilling is done with gentleness. Our fight is won by fleeing to Him. Our implements of war are full of peace. Our warriors are meek and full of grace. Our boot camp begins at birth. Every patient word, every gentle rebuke, every tender touch shapes our children. When we must be firm we are nevertheless kind. And as our babies grow into men and women of God, their ability to wage spiritual battles is dependent upon the faithful drill sergeants who encouraged them to fight against the devil and rebel against the world.

"Be ye in the world.
But not of the world."

DATHAN'S SONG

Welcome now, little stranger
To a world filled with wonder
Filled full of the fragrance
Of life's sweet bouquet
But dear one, take warning
That birth's like a morning
To a lifetime that flies past
Like one single day

Soak up like a sponge
All that's joyful and best
But squeeze yourself out
Upon those who are blessed
A God-given gift
Has been wrapped up in you
You show more of Him
Than I'll ever teach you

Soak up like a sponge
All that's joyful and best
But squeeze yourself out
Upon those who are blessed
A God-given gift
Has been wrapped up in you
You show more of Him
Than I'll ever teach you

There are no words to thank You
For a heart that can see
And gaze in the face
Of this small mystery
You knit him together
In a most secret place
A most certain sign
Of Your wonderful grace

Welcome now, little stranger
To a world filled with wonder
To a world torn asunder
To a world that's in pain
My son, life's a battle
So you be a rebel
Stand ready to fight
And never stop loving the Light

Oh Lord, you have gifted us with a child.

And in so doing You have granted us a chance to embrace what we love.

All that is good and perfect comes from You.
So Father, let the goodness and perfection of this baby draw others to You.
May our child's total dependence *on* us be a lesson *to* us of our complete dependence on You.
Transform our lives to trust You with childlike simplicity.
May the parable of this small life speak to us every day.

Dear Jesus, You are the Life, the Giver of Life, and the Sustainer of Life.
Through You our baby has come to live.
By Your powerful Word this life is sustained.
We ask now that this baby would someday know You as all this and more.
That to this life you would add Life everlasting.

GIFT OF LIFE

JAMES 1:17

Forgive me, O Lord
For being so dim
I've embraced this small gift
Put my arms around him
I was holding so tight
It was all I could do
I forgot that my arms belong
First around You

Now Jesus has taught
To let everything go
All the things that you own
All the people you know
If you'll stop asking questions
And simply obey
You'll possess them
In a much more beautiful way

So sing for the Giver
Whose name is a prayer
And sing to the baby
He's given, so fair
And sing to yourself
Be you husband or wife
And remember a child
Is a gift of Life

May the Lord grant you His peace.

May the One who gave you children
Allow you, by His grace, to become a child again, His child.

May you always have eyes to see the treasure of your baby.

May you be a gift to your child
Even as your child is a gift to you.

May you bless them and
be a blessing.

May they always find in
your arms
the tenderness and comfort
you have found in His.

May they guide you to the
wonder of their world,
As you prepare them for
this present world.

May you always come to the cradle with patience
and peace,
Finding there all the Father has left to be found.

As you sing your baby to sleep,
May you wake up.

In His Name
Amen.

LIGHT OF THE WORLD

You are the Light of the world, oh Lord
(John 8:12)
And You make Your servants shine
So how could there be
Any darkness in me?
If You are the Light of the World
If You are the Light of the World

You are the Bread of Life, oh Lord
(John 6:35)
Broken to set us free
So how could there be
Any hunger in me?
If You are the Bread of Life
If You are the Bread of Life

You've overcome the world, oh Lord
(John 16:33)
And given us victory
So how could I fear
When trouble is near
If You've overcome the world
If You've overcome the world
'Cause you've overcome the world

Morning Prayer

(LAMENTATIONS 3:23)

WE WANTED TO GIVE YOU THIS MORNING, LORD
WE WANTED TO GIVE YOU THIS DAY
THANKS FOR THE SON
AND HIS LIGHT IN OUR HEARTS
THERE ARE SO MANY THINGS WE NEED TO SAY

AS WE LOOK TO A NEW DAY TO SPEND WITH YOU
IT'S EXCITING TO THINK WHAT IT MEANS
THAT YOU WOULD CHOOSE US
AND USE US
AND CALL US YOUR OWN
THAT YOU LOVE US AND GIVE US A NEW SONG TO SING

IN ORDER TO GIVE YOU THE WHOLE OF THE DAY
WE MUST GIVE YOU THIS FIRST SPECIAL PART
THE SUN AS IT RISES REMINDS US OF YOU
A DAY WITHOUT YOU IS
LIKE A DAY IN THE DARK

WE WANTED TO GIVE YOU THIS MORNING, LORD
WE WANTED TO GIVE YOU THIS DAY

There are two ways our children can look at the night.

The first, to see darkness as evil, a token of sin and fallenness.

Jesus said, "This is your hour when darkness reigns" (Luke 22:53).

But there is another way to teach them to see the night.

This point of view looks past the darkness and denies its reign.

"The darkness He called 'night'" (Genesis 1:5).

Why should they fear anything He has called into being and named?

The night is a time for them to remember His name. (Psalm 119:55).

To listen as He sings (Psalm 42:8).

Perhaps even to hear their own names whispered as one unique and

fearless verse.

a song for the night

Like a warm woolen blanket
The dark wraps around
As we cuddle together
And hear all the sounds
Of the night as it's falling
And coming to be
Now look with your ears
Not your eyes, and you'll see

Good night to the trees
So majestic and strong
Good night to the birds
With their wonderful songs
Good night to the planets
That wander above
Good night to a universe
Alive with Your Love

The sounds of the night
Are the notes of a song
So secret and sacred
So beautifully strong
In the air there's an echo
A whisper and a prayer
And though He's not seen
Still the Singer is there

So good night to creation
To the bright shining stars
Good night to the moon
Faithful witness you are
(Psalm 89:37)
Good night to the world
As it hurtles through space
Good night to the wonder
In your shining face

With all that is waiting
The sights and the sounds
Your wonderous world
Like a merry-go-round
Is it any wonder
It's so hard to sleep
While outside You're playing
Your own hide-and-seek

27

Lullaby for Jesus

Baby Jesus please don't cry
Now let me wipe the tears from Your eyes
You cry as though Your heart would break
Please don't spend Your first night awake

Shepherds round You mean no harm
They long to hold You in their arms
To cradle as they might a lamb
But You're too small to understand

Cattle lowing long to sing
A lullaby to soothe their King
A cry so full of pain and fright
That pierces through the lonely night

Baby Jesus please don't cry
Now let me wipe the tears from Your eyes
Baby Jesus please don't weep
For it's night and time for You to sleep

Baby sleeping in the hay
The Son of God who's come to save
The Light, the only Way that's true
Who'll die upon a cross for you.

Baby Jesus please don't weep
It's night and time for You to sleep
The stars that shine don't match the glow
Of all the ones You'll come to know

Oh Father of Jesus

Hold me now
Oh, Father of Jesus
Sheltered, safe,
Asleep in Your arms
No other place
Can promise protection
A fortress from pain
And a haven from harm

Hold me now
Oh, Father of Jesus
Sometimes I fear
The dark of the night
Your kindness kindles
The stars in the heavens
Your love is the reason
The moon gives us light

Just You and I
And one holy moment
Together if I have eyes
That can see
Open my ears
That I might hear You whisper
Of Your tender longing for me

Now I know
Oh, Father of Jesus
My hope lies in
Belonging to You
Never again
Will I live like a stranger
My heart understands now
That You're my Father too

"HE PREDESTINED US TO BE ADOPTED
AS HIS SONS AND DAUGHTERS
THROUGH JESUS CHRIST,
IN ACCORDANCE WITH HIS
PLEASURE AND WILL"
-EPHESIANS 1:5

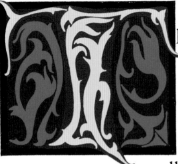here is no place of greater comfort than the arms of your parents. There, fears disappear and tears are dried. There we find, when we are small, a reason to keep going, to brush off the dirt of the playground from bleeding knees and go back to the fray of play, to the fray of life itself.

Mother's arms are comfort and tenderness; father's arms, strength and protection from all that would scare or harm us. Needs drive us to mother. Fear of the world around us drives us to father. God gives us two parents because there are times we need both.

Above and beyond them both is the God whose arms provide all this and more. He is the comfort of mother and the strength of father. Trusting Him is no more than the simple awareness that He is holding you.

Again and again during His time here, Jesus fled to those arms and apparently found there all that He needed to brush off the dirt and go back into the fray of it all. "My Father . . . " He would say, or "your Father . . . " or perhaps best of all, "our Father." His ministry might be summarized as an attempt to make us realize that Father is God's true name and that His greatest hope is to someday hold each one of us.

The comfort that comes from being held is reflected in the face of your child—it is a comfort beyond words, beyond telling, even beyond singing. When you embrace your baby and are tempted to fear for the future of your child, or when you long for that parental embrace yourself, remember that our God, the Father of Jesus, is your Father as well. You, too, are being embraced, but by infinitely stronger arms.